# The WORLD'S STUPIDEST

# I.Q. TEST

Eldon C. Romney

Published by:

Creative Diversions Int'l., Inc.
P.O. Box 9361
Salt Lake City, UT    84109

D1562301

Front cover art, illustration and design by Kerry Soper.
Back cover art, illustration and design by Nobody N. Particular.

The World's Stupidest I.Q. Test
A silly book/May 1992
Creative Diversions/May 1992, Revised, Updated and quite possibly Ruined Version

Library of Congress Catalog Number 92-90238
ISBN  0-9632451-0-4


394  395  396  397  398  399  400  401  402  403

For information or quantity discounts, contact:
Creative Diversions International, Inc.
P.O. Box 9361, Salt Lake City, UT   84109
(801)   466-2019


Over 13 copies sold.
Book trade distribution:   Yeah, right- Only in my dreams.

Printed in the U.S.A.
(In Utah, which generally qualifies)

Serious actual thanks to:


Craig E. Ford,

Larry Matheson,

Clarann Jacobs

and

Tom and Pat Kirkland, dear friends, and Elaine C. Romney, my mother, who believed that my insanity might just be marketable after all, and who invested in it to make this book a reality.

Fictitious thanks to:

DelReigh Preest, DOA

Blaine Cawl, LS, MFT

Louie Slaughton, LM, NOP

**Other authors of this same book:**

Mark Romney Powell, NLBHN; Greg Howes, TLBHN; Irvin Sasaki, TBHN; Vincent C. Romney, OTBHN; Dene Smith, NBHNBTL

**Look for these titles also from this publisher:**

-How to Make $10 in Real Estate

-How to Live Almost Anywhere on $800.00 a Day

-1001 Ways to Increase your Waistline

-Standing Out in a Crowd through Flatulence

-How to Win Phlegms and Influence Pimples

-Tips on Becoming Unemployed

-How to Destroy a Beautiful Relationship

-Achieving Memory Relief

-How to Lose $1,000,000 in the Stock Market

-Thwarting Your Physician

-Favorite Hazardous Wastes

-Earn Your Neighbor's Ire

-A Guide to Weight Loss: Tapeworms and Other Parasites

-Guilt Without Sex:  An Owner's Manual

-Why it Gets Dark at Night and Other Profound Mysteries

# Contents

### Duh!
It's a stupid I.Q. Test, you numbskull!
What on earth did you think?

# Foreward (not Forward, Farword or Foreword)

I.Q. Tests have long been controversial. On the other hand, maybe I.Q. tests have simply been controversial for a long time. But one thing is for certain: the future lies ahead.

This test is a result of many minutes of work and compilation. More than six people have taken this test, and more than one completed it. With any luck, maybe you too will complete it. Some have noticed that there is a feeling of finality once they completed this test. What you notice may be noteworthy. Then again, maybe not.

Perhaps someone soon will pass this test. Presumably they would have to eat it first. If you pay close attention during this test, you will learn something about yourself. And the test. And perhaps about yourself and how you take tests. Or at least how you take this test at this time. Because you could take this test again later (or you could have taken it sooner) and learn something more or less or different than you did this (or last) time, or you could have, and probably did, take other tests previous to this one at other times (and probably at other locations). Or the time before last if you have taken this test more than about twice. Or three times. Possibly four. But I digress. Oh well, nobody reads these parts anyway.

Welcome to the World's Stupidest I.Q. Test. This test will show how you think when you face new problems. It is recommended, therefore, that you think when you face new problems. At least while attempting this test. Which contains new problems. Which it is recommended you think while facing anew.

# Partial List of Tables

| | |
|---|---|
| Dining | Coffee |
| Living Room | Computer |
| Collapsible | Operating |
| Folding | Content |
| Elemental | Picnic |
| Periodic | Logarithmic |
| Multiplication | Conversion |
| Round | Conference |
| Turn | Time |
| End | Occasional |
| Lamp | Water |
| Book | Accessory |
| Dive | Decompression |
| Kitchen | Times |

# Instructions

1. Take out your driver's license or other proof of your identity and draw an exact replica at the top of your answer sheet.

2. Do not use eyeglasses unless you normally wear none, then wear someone else's.

3. Work as fast as you can. Speed will probably help you to score better. At the very least, the more questions you answer, the more answers you will have made when you are finished. Nobody is expected to complete the entire test. You may skip to those questions you mistakenly feel you will do better on.

4. Most people have difficulty with tests and your score will reflect this. All your friends, acquaintances and family members, as well as those who don't care to know you, will be aware how you scored after you take this test. Do your best anyway.

5. You must take this test at one sitting. It is best to cram for this type of test while taking it. Wild guessing will help in some cases, but hurt in others. Tame guessing will not be tolerated.

6. You can take this test only once. You must take it in the order it is numbered. If you do not, you will be cheating. The answer sheet will be computer scored, and the computer can tell if you cheat. And so can your mother.

7. If you are sick, ill, infirmed, have a headache or other extreme or distracting pain, have taken medication which makes you drowsy or sleepy, have had a recent head injury, are very tired or are under excessive emotional or physical stress, or for emotional, physical, spiritual or other reasons cannot concentrate well or for any other reason feel you may not be at your best, I envy you; begin the test immediately.

8. Read only the questions to which you know the answers.

9. Ignore all the directions, including this one, but not the instructions.

10. Please do not write in the test booklet itself. There is an answer sheet located at the back of this book, but don't write on that either- someone else may want not to write on it later also.

P.S. Do you have a stupid question or a stupid answer, or are you just clever or stupid? Write to us: getting mail makes us feel important.

4. Define the universe and give three examples.

719. Two trains are approaching each other at different speeds, originating from different cities within the same state (of the United States). Train B is travelling faster, and Train A is headed in the most northerly direction. Train A departed it's origination city at 1:30 a.m. EST. Train B departed it's destination city at 4:10 a.m. MDT. Assuming cabooses are 39 feet long and hopper cars are 73 feet long, at what time will the caboose on Train A pass the last hopper car in Train B? And why do trains leave at such ridiculous hours?

39. In the question above, why did the airline schedule change for Veteran's Day, but not New Years Day?

True or False?    This is a blank sheet of paper.

1003. A certain item is the envy of all who see it. Explain what it is, who possesses it, critique it from both a philosophical and spiritual standpoint, and write a dissertation on the most important aspect of it. Build a working replica of this item, carefully package it and submit it with your answer sheet following your successful completion of this:

a) debaucle    b) anachronism    c) fiasco    d) tedium

33. Recalculate each problem herein by a factor of 1.00406725.

66. If A + B = C, and A + B + C = D, and A + B + C + D = E, what are the numerical values of A and B?

298. An ocean-going vessel sinks during hostilities in which it was torpedoed. When hit, it was in 1373 feet of water; the vessel is 936 feet long; it takes 7 minutes and 45 seconds for the ship to slip below the surface, and it plummets at at rate of 27 feet per second; the ocean floor is igneous rock.

-Who was on the bridge when the vessel was hit?

-Was this a declared war or just a police action?

-How many people are usually on a 936 foot vessel?

-Did the vessel end up end up?

-What booty did it carry?

-Was there either flotsam or jetsam present?

-And where can you get a plummet?

0. Which word is most descriptive?

999. Write down the best:

Amusement park, college team, professional team, high school team, city to live in, state to live in, world to live in, type of house, type of car, food to eat, food to look at, job to have, job to avoid, friend to have, friend to avoid, person to marry, marital status, vacation spot, discussion topic, word, cleaning solution, book to read, book to avoid reading, clothing to wear, manufacturer's outlet, product, service, store, sickness, roller skate, pant, athlete, animal pet, cat food, cat litter, dog litter, city litter, diaper, cereal, grain, flax, duck feet, politician, supreme being, royalty, ex-spouse, convict, criminal, destruction, worst thing, mechanic, movie, theme, song, movie theme, theme song, movie theme song, stunt man, stunt woman, sex, specie, species, family, genus, genius, phylum, class, order, kingdom, photograph, phonograph, pornograph, Van de Graff, pictograph, autograph, graph paper, newspaper, tissue paper, toilet paper, toilet tissue, theme paper, paper doll, paper chase, paper thing, any thing, thing, non-thing, matter, anti-matter, doesn't matter, does it matter, whatsamatter, etc.

140. Will you enjoy taking this test? May you? Might You? Must you?

107. Are you for or against public opinion?

10. Don't make a decision. What was it?

86. Which two words have the same meaning?

68. Would you enjoy taking this test? Should you enjoy taking this test? Could you enjoy taking this test? Can you, shall you?

94. A man works 8 hours a day, five days a week for many years. When will he retire?

3. Blaine found a small sign on his typewriter which read, "WARNING: Keep fingers, hair, jewelry, etc., from this area." If he finds somebody's shorn-off finger in that area, must he keep it? And is Blaine covered by the law?

56. DelRay has a porcelain seal, given to him by his cherished godmother, which he has just dropped and broken due to a sneeze brought about by his cold. He has a cold remedy which specifically states, "Do not use if seal is broken." What must he do?

48. The following letters, if unscrambled, do not make certain words: **OXFATM** Write them down in the correct order.

25. Billy and Bob each have more money than Jill. Billy tells Bob that if Bob gives him all his money, Billy will have three times what Jill has. Bob tells Billy that if Billy will give him all his money, he won't push his face in. Who ends up with the most money? Explain.

1. What number is precisely one-half to two-thirds the number you might have when you multiply one person's age by the differences in the number of another person's children?

60. Complete the following visual analogy: + is to * as = is to _?

91. Utilizing your three-dimensional visualization, imagine that someone has in their hand a small glass cube. If I take a razor and cut the hand, will the cube

   a) get blood on it?

   b) drop, and if so, will it break, and how many pieces will it break into, if it breaks?

   c) all of the above, with certain exceptions to be named at a sooner date?

23. You have a cough, red bumps on your face and neck and a runny nose. After about three hours, each bump turns blue, festers and begins weeping, and a tightness in your chest grows so intense that you can only breathe with the greatest of difficulty. You become dizzy and nauseous as your wounds throb slowly and insistently. Justify.

33.  You wake up in the hospital, are wracked with pain and can't move a muscle.  What happened?

17.  Do you walk to work, or carry your lunch?

22.  If rainbows were made of sand, would petrolatum be projected?

45.  A man and a woman met on a street.  Who were they and which was older?

77. It was a dark and stormy night. What comes next?

36. A. Who wrote the letter?

88. Do you ever very many of the old folks?

4. Describe in detail how civilization as we know it will end. Prove your work.

101. If BHA damaged DNA and DDT begat PCBs, would LSD and TNT be good for UNMe?

Do 10 of the following to demonstrate your creativity and talent:

1- Carve a usable pair of crutches out of Spam luncheon meat.

2- Lead a symphony of kazoo-playing cockroaches in the 1812 Overture.

3- Make a lifesized map of the United States with prominent landmarks.

4- Make an awardwinning videotape using only mustard and tapeworms.

5- Capture and describe 16 mythical beasts without using vowels.

6- Duplicate all of Michaelangelo's works on 3 X 5 cards with pine gum.

7- Explain in perfect detail why you are taking this test.

8- Build a wheelbarrow out of paper towels and superglue and use it to move Mount Saint Helens to the state of Massachusetts.

9- Using the heat generated by a colony of aardvarks, weld the seams on an army tank you have knitted out of used brillo pads.

73.  Rank the species and races of the earth in order of their intelligence, personality factors and potential for success and happiness.

102.  List all your psychological inadequacies and critique them as Escher would have.

21.  Prove philosophy.

96.  Change the world for the better, win the Nobel Prize, then lead throngs of followers to a useless death in the Namibian deserts. Justify your work.

53. Become obscure and unknown for your life's work. Write a short treatise on how you've wasted your life and its associated feelings. Then burn it. Show your work.

30. "Brothers and sisters have I none. That man's father is my father's son." Why doesn't this person have any brothers or sisters?

45. Disprove and show your work:

    a)     E=emcee squared

    b)     Life

    c)     1+1=2

    d)     Intelligence

89. Using Euclidian Geometry, show that round is an obsolete concept.

26. Connect the blanks to make a sentence: _____ __ _____ __ _

_____ _.

88. How many cups are there in a furlong?

10. Are there more inches in half a year or ounces in a month?

76. How many nergs are in a dok?

54. How many wirkers are there in a rutt?

007. George has a new widget which has a non-productive maniform. If he plugs the intake with a glorfin, must he (or should he) put raybose around the orifice?

172. A new reeble has a flanget on the wrong gaffler. Will it operate as is, and if so what will the power loss be?

40.  A tree falls in the woods.  Who hears it?

2.  Make a list of all the people whose names you do not know.

0.  Duck is to Frog as Bird is to:

   a) plant     b) fungus     c) slime mold     d) one of the above

-29.  Become a millionaire and give it all to charity.  Then go to that charity for help and write the experience in a best selling book whose proceeds again go to charity.  Then tell anyone who will listen how you feel.

17. Rearrange more so it makes a sense the better sentence way of all organizing and grammatically only of following structures:

a- I once was of attractive also like slender you too are a time long ago lithe young supple.

b- suddenly and there was flash of bright a light and blinding overcoming for emotions brilliantly?

c- of ago and nevermore of there sometimes useless rather flaxen many many many thereafter because always!

d- be am is are was were been has have had do does did can could shall should will would may might must.

e- now is the time for all good men to come to the aid of their country.

f- travelling enjoying and of all times fun having many family or friends with we together.

g- ask not what your brain can do for you ask what your brain can do for me.

101. Do not read this.

69. How many fish are there in the Pacific Ocean? Bee's pacific.

90. How many stars are in the Knight Sky?

107. Enter your subconscious mind. Who was that? What were they doing? When did they start? When will they return? Why did they stop?

103. A bullet is fired from a level gun out over the ocean. At the same time, assuming ideal conditions such as no wind, clear blue skies, attractive and willing partner, plenty of money, etc., who will find the bullet first?

a) halibut    b) octopus    c) sea snake    d) crappie    e) skate

111. In the preceeding question, name the ocean and calculate if the speed of the bullet was faster or slower than a level.

8. If 132 people play in a double elimination tennis tournament, how many total games will be played? Remember that about half play doubles, some may default and a few will have ties and rematches.

781. The drawing nearby is in "invisible ink" and only certain people can see it. Identify it and write the answer on the invisible answer space.

drawing>>>>

13. If the above drawing were tilted 90 degrees to the north and laid flat, what would it signify?

71. Your fish has lost its bicycle. What must you do? What should your fish do? And what about the bicycle? What?

71. Jones cannot stand to be near Smith, who hates Johnson, who will not tolerate Jones or Brown, who is disgusted by Jones, Smith and Driggs, who himself is disgusting. If you invite them all to dinner and they sit at the same table, how long before dinner will be served?

28. A is closest to: a) M    b) Z    c) V    d) B    e) some of the above

1. Correct the following until they are spelled write:    a)  naphtha    b) gutteral    c) phlox    d) gargantuan    e) other

43. Describe, in appropriate detail, whether you agree or disagree with the following statement:  "Time was, that what was, was all there was.  That was it.  What would be was not yet, and so also was what wasn't.  What won't be wasn't, isn't and will not be. That is all there is."

18. Thirty men hold a clandestine meeting in a dark, dank cavern somewhere in Asia Minor.  They erect a makeshift altar, as piercing notes are played on a saxophone.  The group dances and performs ritual rites after which they mysteriously skulk away into the accumulating mist.

   a)  Who were these men?

   b)  How high was the altar?

   c)  Where were the women?

   d)  Is this an accurate reflection of reality as they knew it?

   e)  At what age will Asia cease to be a Minor?

   f)  Who, exactly, was pierced by the piercing notes?

   g)  When did this event occur (within 20 minutes)?  Why or why not?

288. Do it once again, but this time do it differently. Insure you get the same result, however. Show your work:




11. When you are lost, which will find you faster? A toppled, rusty weathervane, a sundial struck by lightning, or a compass that points in all directions at the same time? Prove your answer by finding the pot of gold at both ends of a double rainbow.




14. Insert the following names in their proper order in relation to the adjacent names:

    1- John Doe        a)

                        John Doe

                    b)

                        John Doe

                    c)

                        John Doe

                    d)

                        John Doe

                    e)

14. Insert the following names in their proper order in relation to the adjacent names:

2- Jone Golinka    a)

             John Dolinka

             b)

             John Tolinka

             c)

             Juan Bolita

             d)

             Joan Dulinpa

24. You are in a seedy bar and some grizzly old lug like yourself bets you $50 that your heart has only three chambers. With only a pen-knife and a tire iron to assist you, satisfy him that you do indeed have a four chambered heart, if that indeed is the case. Attach a videotape documenting the procedure.

3. Which is most similar?    a) a dog    b) a fish    c) a hamster

136. Look out the window: what is it? If no window, where did it go?

100. Which is bigger, a rock or a ball of string?

16. Two men are given a sandwich and a bicycle. If they leave now, how late will they be?

107. A state has 17 counties with an average of four cities in each county. The largest county has nine cities and the smallest have at least two. What is the median number of cities per county?

6. Prove the existence and non-existence of a supreme being. Show your work in appropriate notation.

60. Three ducks divided by two knives equals_____.

71. Why does your wife/husband/friend/mother/father/other do the things he/she/they do/does?

56. You are sailing off the coast of Alaska; are your Bearings Straight? Show your work in nautical and/or nocturnal form.

52. Which does not belong?   A   Z   H   Y   L

12. You enter a remote cave with only a flashlight, a sandwich and a pack of matches at precisely 8:45 a.m. on a Saturday morning. Fourty-two minutes later, you eat the sandwich.   21 minutes later, you fall into an unmarked cavern, knocking yourself unconscious. When you awaken, you find that you have crushed your left leg, it is pitch black, your flashlight is broken and irrepairable and the matches are soaked beyond hope.   The only movement which does not cause excruciating pain is to rest your left leg upon your right leg, dig your knife into the cave bottom holding it with both hands,   and drag yourself gently along.   You come across an ancient Peloponesian sundial.

  a)  What time is it?

  b)  If so, what color is it?

  c)  Where did the knife come from?

  d)  How did you know?

19. There are 13 pairs of unmatched gloves in a drawer. How many must you take out of the drawer before you can say for certain that you have one pair that fits and coordinates appropriately with your wardrobe?

43. Most nords are twerks and some gronks are twerks and nords, but not all nords, twerks or gronks are friks and very few of the foregoing are gerferkling. What percentage are foregoing?

15. Ursula was only 13 years old when she went through a very traumatic psychological experience. Justify.

43. If a chicken and a half can lay an egg and a half in a day and a half, how long would it take a caterpillar with a wooden leg to kick all the seeds out of a dill pickle?

51. Three servicemen met in the Far East. Each was of a vastly different age and rank and had entered the service at vastly different times. Each has, by now, been married at least once. When they met, the youngest was 3/5 the age of the oldest, the other was 20% older than the youngest, and the youngest had entered the service at the age of 17. The oldest had a heart attack in 1968. The next oldest died in a car wreck at the age of 51.

    a)   How old were they in 1955?

    b)   How many years are in a vast?

    c)   What about Naomi?

    d)   And why not?

27. What is the difference between a duck, if neither wing flaps but the tail?

50. What is the next answer?

20. Fill in the appropriate blanks: _____ __ _____ ____ __ _
_____ .

57. Finish this: / ( -   = + # ^ | ~

5. You are a rebel outlaw set to hang for your alleged crimes. A blood-thirsty mob of over 2000 awaits the spectacle of your death. Calm them and win your release in 21 words or less; you have 30 seconds.

42. Conclusively prove that you are a rational human being in any dead language except Latin.

25. Do not read this question?

11. Do not think of your favorite thing. What is it?

666. Why does water boil at 212 degrees Fahrenheit and freeze at 32 degrees F? Because:

    a-   It is not practical to manufacture longer thermometers.

    b-   The weather's awfully hot when it's 212 and freezing at 32.

    c-   It's also 180 degrees from the North Pole to the South Pole.

    d-   None of the above and the question's wrong too.

1413. What is your favorite color? Justify why it is cobalt and describe why it is flying.

70. Where does a sun cause sunburn, a moon moonshine, and a star stardust? Support your answers with photographs.

5. Who is a monsoon?

   a- A year that is short one month.

   b- A gentle Frenchman.

   c- An oon protuberating on a mons.

   d- An Oklahoman who is not quick enough?

$- The amount of money you will send to the editor of this test will
   be:      a)    vast

            b)    enourmous

            c)    huge

            d)    only large

6. Why is there not more of the things that if there was more of
   them there would be more of the things that more people would
   be more happy with and less of the things that more people seem
   to be less happy with more of the time?

^)- Which word is most familiar?

    a)     triune

    b)     naphtha

    c)     redolent

    d)     ululate

@- It has been said that time flies like an eagle, and fruit flies like a banana. What does a just plane fly like?

+- Milk is to anger as debris is to:

    a)     enough

    b)     walk

    c)     tailor

    d)     punt

!- Pick the right antonyms for these two underlined words:

Missing:   not here; unpresent; gone; unknown

Slender:   skinny; thin; unmassive; slight

Pleased:   happy; joyful; contented; satisfied

#- Which of the following is most desirable for you?

a)   Thermonuclear  conflagration

b)   Genocide

c)   Total  anhialation

d)   Mesothelioma

4- Why or why not?

&- Which of the following do you find most appealing?

a) Fratricide

b) Amputation

c) Execution

d) Brain stem death


%- Help is to maintenance as increase is to:

a) uncle

b) sister

c) mother

d) another uncle

e) another mother

f) it depends

(Hint: it does not depend)

*- Rash is to honest as silence is to:

a)  Offend

b)  Ounce

c)  Nose

d)  Mammal

;- Match the words in the first column to the words which are closest in meaning from the second column.

| Excruciating pain | Marriage |
| Slowly dying | Employment |
| Traumatic shock | The opposite sex |
| Hell on earth | Sex itself |

:- Match the words in the first column to the words which are closest in meaning from the second column.

Nirvana                     Decapitation

Heaven                      Thumb screws

Sheer ecstasy               The rack

Exceeding pleasure          Chinese water torture

1. You will be given something of great value and importance. What is it? When will you get it? What will you do with it? Why will you do or not do what it is you should do or should not do that you could do or could not do?

Now write four difficult (or impossible) questions on your own. They will be graded the same as the previous questions.

98. A group of 52 sixteen to seventeen year-old cheerleaders are loaded onto a Boeing 727 aircraft in New York City. They are excitedly yakking, chattering and carrying on characteristic of girls their age. You are scheduled on the same flight after a 32-hour drinking binge at the Lotus Flower Lounge that started on the heels of a devastating trade show appearance where your new invention failed to muster anything but sneers, outright laughter and pointed criticism. Assuming winds are negligible, a full fuel load and a parasite drag coefficient of .0075 N, at what time will you remove the machine gun you smuggled aboard from the overhead compartment and open fire, while screaming the titles of Zamfir's last 20 world famous hits?

   a.   Can't be figured without knowing density of JP-4 jet fuel.

   b.   Only the lonely....

   c.   Yes

   d.   126.4 KHz

22. Using your knowledge of Newtonian mechanics, finish this sentence: Ab farb nogort, kijigo morgofnik...

Solve this equation for Z:   $\underline{AxY+BmF-2TrRx\{45y-X3\}}$
                              $3\{9[12Cb]2M+7DXE\}Y-F5L$

Harry tears the wings off a fly. Reveal how far it must travel for its next meal, what the extent of the meal will be and determine what the fly now should most appropriately be called.

How many grains of sand make a beach, stars make a night sky, rocks make a mountain and how long must something be before it reaches far?

# EXTRA CREDIT

S- Capture some Zero Gravity and secure it on your answer sheet.

T- Travel back in time, meet yourself, and attach proof of your identities on your answer sheet.

U- Do not think of a Purple Cow.

P- Define love in the perfect sense so all humanity will agree.

I- Which object on your right could be cut, flattened, smashed, welded and shaped into the object at my left?

D- Which one of the objects on the right might be cut, flattened, smashed, welded and shaped into the abject at my left?

T- The following is a familiar phrase in the ancient Ho-Pek language.
   "Mlkiav ytamd    gudli  numnut."
   What does the following say?    "Uradmfrot"

E- You visit a doctor because you've felt sluggish and morose. He gives you a physical, draws some blood and takes other necessary samples, screens them and then tells you it is imperative you have this prescription filled within 30 minutes or you face certain death:

   ·¥©˙©ƒ®†ø¬¬ππø¨¥©ƒ∑ßç©∫µ≤≥√ƒ®¥

   At the pharmacy, the Pharmacist says the doctor's writing is unclear. What does it say? Will you die? From what? And what can you learn from the doctor's handwriting? And do you have to take the prescription or just fill it to survive?

S- Fill in the dots and determine the species:    :.:...:::....

T- Successfully complete this puzzle:    N.B.

# DOUBLE DARE EXTRA CREDIT

=- Pick ten of the following words which most closely apply to you:
drab, feeble, inept, incompetent, hapless, dull, ordinary, fat, wierd, obstinate, extreme, puny, resistant, loose, careless, cheap, false, odd, poor, ruthless, ugly, slow, destitute, desperate, sinful, wrong, unkind, hopeless, boring, disgusting, stupid, worthless, imbalanced, dangerous, insipid, obscure, insignificant, pathetic.

/- While visiting Japan, you purchase a ticket for the "Bullet Train" or "Shin" (short for Shinkansen) as it is known locally. Travelling at just over 204 kilometers per hour, the train is heading north toward Tokyo, but you are facing south, eating in the dining car. You choke on a piece of rice. A well-intentioned gentleman approaches you from behind, performing the Heimlich maneuver on you, dislodging the rice and expelling it from your mouth. What is its velocity in relation to the ground?

l- Still riding the Shin, you have taken your seat and are now facing forward. At 212 kph, your train collides with another, mistakenly travelling at exactly the same speed in the opposite direction and on the same track. As the dust settles, which of these best describes you?

> a) Bul-go-gi
> b) Teppan yaki
> c) Shabu shabu
> d) Dozo

\- Given pernicious countenance causation behind the perspicatious clientele, you calculate the diminutive condecentions neither beleaguer not perceptibly impact the position in the negative, which of these: slug; snail; worm; octopus beak

This has been a test. If this had been only a drill, you could have heard a whirring noise when the drill was turned on. But this was only a test. Nothing to get turned on by, unless perhaps you're a member of Mensa or one of the other highly intelligent groups, or are just an intelligent individual, or for that matter, unless you just get turned on by tests, which is something else altogether. Altogether is rather, or approximately, like entirely, incidentally. Kind of.

How stupid are you?  Check this graph to find out:

```
9

8

7

6

5

4

3

2

1

0
     0    1    2    3    4    5    6    7    8    9
```

How did you do?  How will you do?  How do you do?  What did you do?  Who will you do?  Who will you know?  Who do you know? How do you know?  How will you know?  How didn't you know? What didn't you know?  What don't you know?  Why not, you know?  When will you know?  Why don't you know?

# ANSWER SHEET
## ANSWER SHEET
### ANSWER SHEET
ANSWER SHEET
ANSWER SHEET
ANSWER SHEET

Write all answers in chronological order:

Send to: W.S.I.Q.T., P.O. Box 9361, Salt Lake City, UT 84109-0361
with small, unmarked bills:  we may get back to you.

# Appendix

Specifically known as the vermiform (having the form of a worm) appendix [anatomy], a small blind sac projecting from the cecum (also spelled caecum; the blind end of the sac at the beginning of the large intestine).

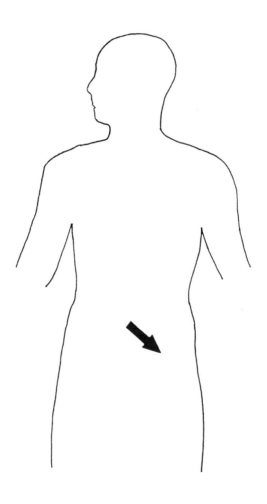

# Index

# Concordance

1. Τακε ουτ ψουρ δριϖερ϶σ λιχενσε ορ οτηερ προοφ οφ ψουρ ιδεντιτψ ανδ δραω αν εξαχτ ρεπλιχα ατ τηε τοπ οφ ψουρ ανσωερ σηεετ.

2. Δο νοτ υσε εψεγλασσεσ υνλεσσ ψου νορμαλλψ ωεαρ νονε, τηεν ωεαρ σομεονε ελσεσ.

3. Ωορκ ασ φαστ ασ ψου χαν. Σπεεδ ωιλλ προβαβλψ ηελπ ψου το σχορε βεττερ. Ατ τηε ϖερψ λεαστ, τηε μορε θυεστιονσ ψου ανσωερ, τηε μορε ανσωερσ ψου ωιλλ ηαϖε μαδε ωηεν ψου αρε φινισηεδ. Νοβοδψ ισ εξπεχτεδ το χομπλετε τηε εντιρε τεστ. Ψου μαψ σκιπ το τηοσε θυεστιονσ ψου μιστακενλψ φεελ ψου ωιλλ δο βεττερ ον.

4. Μοστ πεοπλε ηαϖε διφφιχυλτψ ωιτη τεστσ ανδ ψουρ σχορε ωιλλ ρϵφλϵχτ τηισ Αλλ ψουρ φριενδσ, αχθυαιντανχεσ ανδ φαμιλψ μεμβερσ, ασ ωελλ ασ τηοσε ωηο δον϶τ χαρε το κνοω ψου, ωιλλ βε αωαρε ηοω ψου σχορεδ αφτερ ψου τακε τηισ τεστ. Δο ψουρ βεστ ανψωαψ.

5. Ψου μυστ τακε τηισ τεστ ατ ονε σιττινγ. Ιτ ισ βεστ το χραμ φορ τηισ τψπε οφ τεστ ωηιλε τακινγ ιτ. Ωιλδ γυεσσινγ ωιλλ ηελπ ιν σομε χασεσ, βυτ ηυρτ ιν οτηερσ. Ταμε γυεσσινγ ωιλλ νοτ βε τολερατεδ.

6. Ψου χαν τακε τηισ τεστ ονλψ ονχε. Ψου μυστ τακε ιτ ιν τηε ορδερ ιτ ισ νυμβερεδ. Ιφ ψου δο νοτ, ψου ωιλλ βε χηεατινγ. Τηε ανσωερ σηεετ ωιλλ βε χομπυτερ σχορεδ, ανδ τηε χομπυτερ χαν τελλ ιφ ψου χηεατ. Ανδ σο χαν ψουρ μοτηερ.

7. Ιφ ψου αρε σιχκ, ιλλ, ινφιρμεδ, ηαϖε α ηεαδαχηε ορ οτηερ εξτρεμε ορ διστραχτινγ παιν, ηαϖε τακεν μεδιχατιον ωηιχη μακεσ ψου δροωσψ ορ σλεεπψ, ηαϖε ηαδ α ρεχεντ ηεαδ ινφυρψ, αρε ϖερψ τιρεδ ορ αρε υνδερ εξχεσσιϖε εμοτιοναλ ορ πηψσιχαλ στρεσσ, ορ φορ εμοτιοναλ, πηψσιχαλ, σπιριτυαλ ορ οτηερ ρεασονσ χαννοτ χονχεντρατε ωελλ ορ φορ ανψ οτηερ ρεασον φεελ ψου μαψ νοτ βε ατ ψουρ βεστ, βεγιν τηε τεστ ιμμεδιατελψ.

8. Ρεαδ ονλψ τηε θυεστιονσ το ωηιχη ψου κνοω τηε ανσωερσ.

9. Ιγνορε αλλ τηε διρεχτιονσ, ινχλυδινγ τηισ ονε, βυτ νοτ τηε ινστρυχτιονσ.

# <u>Glossary</u>

# THIS IS YOUR BRAIN

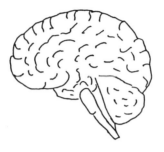

# THIS IS YOUR BRAIN ON DUH.

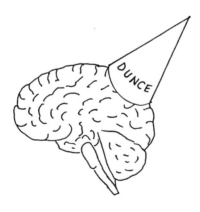

# DON'T DO DUH!

"Winners don't do duh." _William Emissions, CIA, FBI, EPA, HEPA

Eldon C. Romney is a male human who was born in Hot Springs National Park, Arkansas in 1953. He is the son of an Air Force (formerly Army Air Corps) pilot. He grew up (at least physically) in Salt Lake City, Utah, and attended Skyline High School, where he became known as a tremendously mediocre student. He had a draft number of 26, and subsequently joined the Army to see the world. He saw Fort Ord, California and Fort Carson, Colorado, as an infantryman, carpenter and clerk. He earned the National Defense Service Medal, the Good Conduct Medal, and the Army Commendation Medal. He unknowingly donated his knees to the Army medical practice, a move which helped him through college at the University of Utah. He actually graduated with, appropriately, a B.S. He has worked as a Federal Investigator, a City/County Health Department worker, an Employment Interviewer, a salesman, an entrepreneur, and an environmental and asbestos consultant. He is an EPA accredited instructor for AHERA (asbestos) courses and has taught those courses in the Western United States, Japan, Okinawa and Korea. He believes he has worked as an author. He has been married and divorced more times than he likes to admit, and has fathered two girls, who actually seem to tolerate him fairly well. He belongs to American Mensa (the High I.Q. Society) and has held positions in the Utah and national organizations, including Proctor, which is to say, Qualification Test Administrator. There are actually some local charitable organizations which have allowed him to either be on their boards of directors or help out in other ways. Personally, I don't know if I would go that far. You see, he's not a died-in-the-wool Republican. He's kindof an independent. And you know what that means.

-The President of the Untied States, May 1992

CHECK THE APPROPRIATE SPACES:

__ O.K., I'll bite; send me another copy of

## The World's Stupidest I.Q. Test

Enclosed is my remittance (U. S. money) of $4.95 plus one dollar and five cents ($1.05) postage and handling, totalling (my choice):

__ $6.00

__ $9.69

__ $22.50

for each book.

I understand I'll get my book(s) in about 5 weeks or so.

Send the book(s) to:

Name_____

Address_____

City, State, Zip_____

__ Thank you very, very much          Send this form to:

__ Thank you                          Creative Diversions Int'l. Inc.

__ Just send the book(s)              POB 9361, SLC, UT  84109

**Guarantee**: If you are not completely satisfied with this book, please feel free to return it to the publisher with our compliments, absolutely free of obligation. Simply include a check or money order for $15.98 (U.S.) to cover handling, restocking fees and emotional trauma to the author. Residents of foreign countries and Utah please enclose International Postal Reply Coupon worth $14.69 (U.S.). All others please enclose a self addressed stamped #17 envelope (white or lavender), three negotiable stock certificates and small silver bars weighing at least twelve (12) avoirdupois ounces (336 g.). If you have lived west of the International Date Line at any time in the past 156 months, also enclose ten or more solid gold coins for each vowel in your full name. Others send unmarked genuine U.S. currency equal in weight to their primary mode of transportation or spouse, which ever is more. Upon receipt, we will begin to start to try to endeavor to find your file.